ATOMIC POWER OF FASTING

ATOMIC POWER OF FASTING

DR. EVETTE YOUNG

© Copyright 2021—Dr. Evette Young. All rights reserved.

This book is protected under the copyright laws. This book may not be copied or reprinted for commercial gain or profit. The use of short quotations or occasional page copying for personal or group study is permitted and encouraged. Permission will be granted upon request. Unless otherwise identified, Scripture quotations are taken from the King James Version. All emphasis within Scriptures is the author's own.

Please note that Royal Publishers™ publishing style capitalizes certain pronouns in Scripture that refer to the Father, Son, and Holy Spirit, and may differ from some Bible publishers' styles. Take note that the name satan and related names are not capitalized. We choose not to acknowledge him, even to the point of violating grammatical rules.

Due to the revelatory content of this material and because of the author's commitment to preserve the integrity and personal reading experience, editorial license was taken to maintain the spiritual and physical impact of the underlining subjects revealed in this book.

This book and all other Royal Publisher™ books are available at Christian bookstores and distributors worldwide. To order products, or for any other correspondence:

ROYAL PUBLISHER™ USA Email:
media@transformationisnow.org Or reach us on the
Internet: www.transformationisnow.org
ISBN 13: 979-8-3303-7543-1
ISBN 13 EBOOK: 979-8-3303-7544-8

For Worldwide Distribution, Printed in the U.S.A.

Dedication

This book is dedicated to my mother; Evelyn W. Young, who modeled a fasting lifestyle before my eyes from childhood to adulthood. She remains my first example of a committed life of sacrificial fasting. Today my Mother is 77 years young, and still practicing fasting. I witness her devotion to prayer and fasting, and I truly know, and I believe it is what saved my life on many occasions. She stood on the Word of the LORD, declaring, Me and my household shall be saved. I love my dearest Mother!

Acknowledgements

Special thanks to:

My husband Apostle (Dr.) John King Hill and my precious daughter Anointed Evelyn-Divine, for all your support and encouragements.

My Father and mother: Mr. & Mrs. Emmanuel and Evelyn Young for their many years of hard work and supporting me!

Dr. D. K. Olukoya, Mountain of Fire, Nigeria, West Africa.

Pastor Rod Parsley, World Harvest Church, Columbus, Ohio.

Apostle Victor Ronnie Nnamdi, Nigeria, West Africa.

Table of Contents

Fasting 01

Types of Fasting 08

Acceptable and Effective Fasting 25

Building Up Your Faith 31

Lengths and Types of Fast 37

Checking Your Heart 41

Power Tools 47

Meditation and Rest 55

Angels and Warfare 62

Fasting for Freedom 68

Author's Note to Reader

I would like to personally thank you for purchasing this material. For many years I carried this book with you in mind. I am grateful to the LORD for giving me grace to birth this project through much prayer and intercession for the reader. I know God has wonderful things in store for your life, and this book will facilitate your reality. When I began my fasting journey, I saw the LORD move in powerful ways. I learned that prayer alone at times won't hit the target. I was among those who had a "This Kind" type of situation in my life. (See Matthew 17:21). My life would have been swallowed up if I did not adhere to the Biblical practice of Fasting and Prayer. I believe the End Times Church will walk in dynamic power by crucifying her flesh so the Glory of the LORD God will be revealed to the dark world. You must not forget that you are the salt of the earth, and the light of the world. As you continue to yield your heart to the King of kings and LORD of lords, He will use you to participate in the Great Harvest and end times revival and exploits. I commend you, and I'm cheering you on as you journey deeper into the realms of the Spirit.

Beginning Prayer For Reader

Father in the mighty name of Jesus Christ, we plead the blood of Jesus over our lives, families, and everything attached to us. As I dive into this dynamic material, I pray that everything you intend to transpire in my life will manifest. Provide us with the courage, strength and push that it will take to pursue the practice and discipline of fasting and prayer. We know that it is not by might, nor by power but by your Spirit. It is mandatory for us to know your voice; therefore, help me by revealing your hidden truths that will alter the course of my life and give me the power to overcome all obstacles, snares, and works of darkness. I invite you Holy Spirit to help me on this journey and remove every wall and obstruction in my way. Open my spiritual eyes to see my divine victory in the mighty name of Jesus Christ. Amen.

Forward

If there is any time in the history of mankind's existence that is full of uncertainties, it's now. That's why we all have to avail ourselves to all that heaven has provided us, which can enable us to beat the odds in three realms, spirit, soul, and materially. For that reason, I am proudly introducing to you one of the 21st century's prepared vessels of the LORD in the person of Dr. Evette J. Young. She has meticulously put together a written weapon that many of us have not harnessed for such a long time. Captioned "The Atomic Power of Fasting." A work of love and strenuous experience that fits the narrative of our day and times. Make sure to get a hold of this book and experience a major difference in your spiritual life and walk with the Almighty God in the End Times.

Thank you,
Apostle Victor Bessong
Hour of Celebration Netword International Inc.,
Brockton, MA. USA

Preface

Throughout years of my personal experiences, prayer has become a part of my life. Some challenges offered me no other options; therefore, I had to adjust regardless of pressures. Sometimes, we attend to prayers from a religious or casual approach but it is rather a key to solving deep humanitarian problems. Besides, the surface overviews of petitioning and requesting for answers to our basic needs, prayer opens to deeper mysteries. By taking the time to embrace the process and carefully uncover the secrets to spiritual dialogues, other areas of prayers suddenly begin to unfold to usher us into unchartered territories.

All prayers are not equal and we must carefully envision quality and values in our interpretations of prayers. Expectation for personal results can be a motivational factor, but cultivating a prayer life takes more than getting a victory or receiving a blessing. Life is what brings order because normalcy means removing other attachments and irregularities. A passion to do something is different from a heart pressing burden and the same applies to a deeper longing for a life beyond the norms.

It is why hunger and thirst help drive us to seek after the LORD. Our passion can create limitations or obscure our desires to experience life above our immediate needs. Anything that is permanent is superior over those things that last for a period. Prayer has revolutionized my life to a point that I have come to realize it is the wheel, which fans the speed of life. In my years of observing different phases of interacting with God through prayers, I have gained insights that are more valuable than all other subjects. We have to see prayer as a higher curriculum because whatever induces acceleration also gives life the wings to project above known or familiarized boundaries.

This is why prayer is closing the gaps between beliefs, hope, and trust — what things ever you desire, when you pray.... A conclusion is better than anticipation. If we only know that prayer releases the keys of spiritual trajectories to unlock our stagnated lives into motions, some of us would pray in seasons and out of seasons. A burden is like adding flavors to a recipe; however, someone who knows how to put the recipes together must prepare the meal. The satisfaction of prayer cannot be judged only by answers to prayers, so we must look at the sacrifices like putting different ingredients together.

A hunger, thirst, and burden are ingredients that regulate the passion to consummate a lifestyle of prayer. Instead of expectations to receive, I have achieved the adjustments to wait upon the LORD. Most importantly, I have also learned to treasure the importance of dialogue and intimacy rather than exchanging my communications for the sake of receiving the rewards. I want to know Him — I want to know what is in His heart and other addendum or requirements, so I value relationship above spending time to get something. I am searching for Him more than talking to Him for a price. My prayers are no longer price quotes and my expectations are His heart above His answers.

Seeking after Him is more to me than buying and selling. My values for prayers have increased: Jesus said, I know you hear me all the time. In this Book, I am offering you more than a therapy.

I am giving you an opportunity for a seat-down adventure to experiment beyond religious concerts and auditions, and explore different sides of prayers that value so much to life.

As you dive in, I want you to forget about the old ways of engaging in prayers and open yourself to experience the dynamics of deeper realms of prayers. Desires are the beginning of passion but life offers more than personal gratifications. You need a vibrant prayer life above answer to prayers or your ability to wait upon the LORD will dry up like a desert. I pray for a turning point in your walk with the LORD as you navigate this material. I am believing for a supernatural testimony in your life.

In His Service,
Dr. Evette Young.

Chapter One

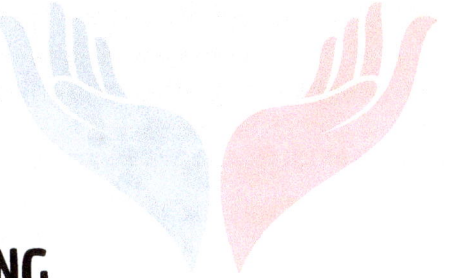

FASTING

Fasting can be seen as abstinence from all or some kinds of food or drink, especially as a religious observance.

And God said, let us make man in our image, after our likeness: and let them have dominion over the fish of the sea, and over the fowl of the air, and over the cattle, and over all the earth, and over every creeping thing that creepeth upon the earth (Genesis 1:26).

The above Scripture verse is an important part of building our foundation because of the implication – God's intention as it relates to the architectural design of man. God made/created man in His Image After His Likeness.

We understood from Scriptures that the LORD God (Elohim) is one person -- operating in distinctive personifications. We can also establish similar mysteries with man! I used the word "similar" to point out that something shifted after the fall. Man is made a spirit, soul, and body (or the triune nature of man).

The similarity is found in the activities within the component of his being. There was WHOLENESS and oneness, which are parts of completion and perfection.

After the fall, the different components of human makeup entered a phase of internal struggle – a continuous war between the spirit and the flesh. The flesh became man's greatest undoing! The Bible said, the flesh war against the spirit. You may ask, what about the soul? The soul became part of the battleground for spiritual warfare.

The following Scriptures will help us to look more closely into the dynamics:

Apostle Peter wrote, dearly beloved, I beseech you as strangers and pilgrims, abstain from fleshly lusts, which war against the soul (1 Peter 2:11).

Paul said, there is therefore now no condemnation to them which are in Christ Jesus, who walk not after the flesh, but after the Spirit (Romans 8:1).

That the righteousness of the law might be fulfilled in us, who walk not after the flesh, but after the Spirit (Romans 8:4).

This I say then, walk in the Spirit, and ye shall not fulfill the lust of the flesh (Galatians 5:16).

If we live in the Spirit, let us also walk in the Spirit (Galatians 5:25).

Romans 8:1 indicates that something significant took place: the flesh became a standalone while the spirit is separated and the soul is locked in-between. In other words, the soul can easily tilt toward the spirit or flesh! Every decision a man makes happens within the soul. The soul responds to the signals from both the flesh and spirit.

Our physical body (the skin) is not of a carnal nature! It is only a product of the carnal nature (fallen man). This is why carnality is fed through the lusts of the flesh. Your heavenly tabernacle, which is going to be a new glorified body, is more in tune with the dictates of the spirit.

Psalms 82:6 made this powerful statement: I have said, Ye are gods; and all of you are children of the Most High.

As God's kind, "Image after His Likeness" the abilities and capabilities -- the possibilities in Christ are parts of our inheritance.

Blessed be the God and Father of our Lord Jesus Christ, who hath blessed us with all spiritual blessings in heavenly places in Christ (Ephesians 1:3).

If the Scriptures stated that we are His "Image After His Likeness" and our heavenly Father has BLESSED us with all spiritual blessings in the heavenly places in Christ, what we need therefore are access into the heavenly realms and dimensions to possess our inheritance in Christ!

The Bible said, but the natural man receives not the things of the Spirit of God: for they are foolishness unto him: neither can he know them, because they are spiritually discerned (1 Corinthians 2:14).

The greatest problem with spirituality is carnality! What is our option? We must graduate from natural man to spiritual man. It is important to understand that the process takes compliance to achieve the transition.

If a carnal man is going to access his or her spiritual blessings in Christ, he or she must embrace a spiritual change and transformation to complete the process. Although God loves us, He restrains the carnal man from accessing certain spiritual treasures. I am sure that as a careful and responsible parent, you would not simply release the car keys to your 5 years old son or daughter to get behind the wheel and drive?

The reason is because even if the child is intelligent enough to start up the vehicle, he or she may lack the mental readiness to drive safely. Therefore, we can draw a conclusion that the child will inevitably be involved in a dangerous accident with unpredictable consequences. Because you love your child, you will do everything in your power to protect the car keys until he or she reaches the age of accountability and responsibility. Age is part of maturity but growth embodies certain qualifications or ability.

Now I say, That the heir, as long as he is a child, differeth nothing from a servant, though he be lord of all(Galatians 4:1).

To break free from the limitations of the flesh and the impact on the soul, God uses fasting and prayers as curriculum to train and equip us. Fasting is not an elective but a core part of our spiritual growth and maturation. Without fasting and prayer whether periodically or continuously, you will incur numerous delays because of carry overs. Spiritual timings, seasons, and moments take precision or you will miss the windows, doors, and gates of opportunities.

Some basic necessities are available, often without us having to fast and pray: salvation for example is a free gift from God because of the finished works of Jesus Christ on the cross. However, the application processes of salvation take work – you need collaboration with the Holy Spirit to realize the provision in your life.

People fast everywhere across the world from different religious standpoints, nevertheless, acceptable kingdom fasting begins when you know Jesus Christ as your personal Savior and LORD.

Is not this the fast that I have chosen? to loose the bands of wickedness, to undo the heavy burdens, and to let the oppressed go free, and that ye break every yoke? Is it not to deal thy bread to the hungry, and that thou bring the poor that are cast out to thy house? when thou seest the naked, that thou cover him; and that thou hide not thyself from thine own flesh? Then shall thy light break forth as the morning, and thine health shall spring forth speedily: and thy righteousness shall go before thee; the glory of the LORD shall be thy rereward (Isaiah 58:6-8).

Chapter Two

TYPES OF FASTING

When it comes to fasting, there are no rigid rules or formulas on how to fast. Nevertheless, you must learn to follow the leadership of the Holy Spirit. This will help you to adopt the necessary requirement for your type of fast per time.

Here are some biblical types of fasting:

DANIEL'S 10 DAYS APPROACH TO FASTING:

Prove thy servants, I beseech thee, ten days; and let them give us pulse to eat, and water to drink.

So, he consented to them in this matter, and proved them ten days.

And at the end of ten days their countenances appeared fairer and fatter in flesh than all the children which did eat the portion of the king's meat (Daniel 1:12, 14, and 15).

Daniel's exercise required discipline. It was against his custom to eat the king's food dedicated to idols.

He asked for permission:

To eat only vegetables and drink water! He knew that his spiritual adventures with God would produce a healthier outlook than those feeding on food sacrificed to idols.

He was granted his request and the difference was compared after ten days of careful observation. Vegetables and water are not all that made his fasting effective, there was a degree of the element of the Spirit. The radiation was evident of spiritual change and transformation over his life.

You may also remember how the face of Moses shone bright after his return from the mountain top. (See Exodus 34:29-30). These experiences are for the people of God today, and now is the time for you to begin your spiritual adventure with God through fasting.

DANIEL'S 21 DAYS OF FASTING

Then he said unto me, Fear not, Daniel: for from the first day that didst set thine heart to understand, and to chasten thyself before thy God, thy words thou were heard, and I am come for thy words. But the prince of the kingdom of Persia withstood me one and twenty days: but, lo, Michael, one of the chief princes, came to help me; and I remained with the kings of Persia (Daniel 10:12-13).

The challenge with Daniel was not God because He already dispatched the response to his travail. However, opposing powers stood against the release. The great news is that he persisted until the answer came. This same scenario applies to us today. Powers are contending for our blessings even when we are unaware of the circumstances. It is important to see the need for fasting and remaining in prayers always! Daniel waited in fasting and prayers until 21 days instead of stopping after a few days.

For we wrestle not against flesh and blood, but against principalities, against powers, against the rulers of the darkness of this world, against spiritual wickedness in high places (Ephesians 6:12).

The key secret about fasting is that it can give you an advantage in spiritual warfare. There are levels and dimensions of warfare, and we must not become careless. Although our warfare is not against people, there are those influenced negatively by spirits.

KING DARIUS' FAST

Then the king went to his palace, and passed the night fasting: neither were instruments of music brought before him: and his sleep went from him (Daniel 6:18).

There are a number of factors that can impact the zeal of people to fast: number one is when our lives are threatened or under attacks! The dimension of light that Daniel hosted in his life caused the king to like him. He did not know that his decree was meant to target Daniel. Had he known he would not have fallen for the crafty deception. A king's order cannot go without implementation.

There is something to note here: In the king's fast, instruments of music were removed from him. Our churches are filled with indulgence today. We entertain ourselves and loose the presence of God. We deprive ourselves the discipline to engage the LORD and therefore, forfeit the answers to our fasting and prayers. We sabotage the move of God and make false edicts and empty proclamations.

You cannot mix pleasure with sacrifices and yet experience the real power of God. I am convinced that according to the custom of the kingdom, the kings are entertained with quality music until they go to bed. However, the king sacrificed the pleasure because of his burden. He wanted to keep away all distractions and focus only on the purpose of his fast.

Spiritual exercises are not so easy as some people may assume; therefore, you want to carefully maximize the grace of God and disconnect from all distractions!

Let me give you spiritual advice: you must learn to separate your sacrifices from other pleasures. You must keep away distractions when you are fasting and praying to the

LORD including but not limited to social media, mobile games, chatting or unnecessary outings, etc. For married couples you may want to wait until after fasting before sexual contacts.

Paul wrote: Defraud ye not one the other, except it be with consent for a time, that ye may give yourselves to fasting and prayer; and come together again, that Satan tempt you not for your incontinency (1 Corinthians 7:5).

Married couples can negotiate and set the terms for sexual contacts during the periods of fasting and prayers. You and your spouse can work out an agreement or arrangement. If your marriage partner is godly, he or she will understand the reason for such sacrifice. From King Darius' fast, we can learn how important it is to subscribe to minimum comfort during our periods of fasting and prayers.

JONAH'S FAST

Now the word of the LORD came unto Jonah the son of Amittai, saying, Arise, go to Nineveh, that great city, and cry against it; for their wickedness is come up before me. But Jonah rose up to flee unto Tarshish from the presence of the LORD, and went down to Joppa; and he found a ship going to Tarshish: so, he paid the fare thereof, and went down into it, to go with them unto Tarshish from the presence of the LORD. But the LORD sent out a great wind into the sea, and there was a mighty tempest in the sea, so that the ship was likely to be broken (Jonah 1:1-4).

Jonah rejected God's command and the consequences were extremely difficult. These Scripture verses may sound like poems but they are records of adventures with God. Could you imagine what life looked like for Jonah in the belly of the fish?

Our disobedience has much to do with the weaknesses of our fleshly desires. Jonah's fast was compulsory – he had no food or grocery stores and supermarkets around him. I want to point out how God used the circumstances to deal with his soul. When we are fasting and praying, we are not doing God any favor! We are rather subjecting our souls to align with His Spirit.

Then Jonah prayed unto the LORD his God out of the fish's belly, and said, I cried by reason of mine affliction unto the

LORD, and he heard me; out of the belly of hell cried I, and thou heardest my voice. For thou hadst cast me into the deep, in the midst of the seas; and the floods compassed me about: all thy billows and thy waves passed over me. Then I said, I am cast out of thy sight; yet I will look again toward thy holy temple. The waters compassed me about, even to the soul: the depth closed me round about, the weeds were wrapped about my head. I went down to the bottoms of the mountains; the earth with her bars was about me forever: yet hast thou brought up my life from corruption, O LORD my God. When my soul fainted within me, I remembered the LORD: and my prayer came in unto thee, into thine holy temple (Jonah 2:1-7).

Jonah went without food and water for three days and nights. He was completely isolated from the external environment. He was closed in with God. It took three days and nights for the purging of his soul! You may want to consider Jonah's kind of fast when you begin to notice traces of sin pressuring you to disobey God. It is said that desperate times require desperate measures! Repentance, a broken spirit, turning from sin, and asking God for forgiveness will cause His mercy to fall upon your life.

And the LORD spoke unto the fish, and it vomited out Jonah upon the dry land (Jonah 2:10).

EZRA'S FAST

Then I proclaimed a fast there, at the river of Ahava, that we might afflict ourselves before our God, to seek of him a right way for us, and for our little ones, and for all our substance. For I was ashamed to require of the king a band of soldiers and horsemen to help us against the enemy in the way: because we had spoken unto the king, saying, the hand of our God is upon all them for good that seek him; but his power and his wrath is against all them that forsake him. So, we fasted and besought our God for this: and he was intreated of us (Ezra 8:21-23).

Ezra sought the LORD through fasting, and He heard and answered. If you seek Him with a sincere heart, you will find Him! God is not a man that He should lie, and neither the son of man that He should repent.

FASTING ACCORDING TO LENGTH OF TIME

24 HOURS FAST (one day)

And they mourned, and wept, and fasted until even, for Saul, and for Jonathan his son, and for the people of the LORD, and for the house of Israel; because they were fallen by the sword (2 Samuel 1:12).

72 HOURS FAST (three days)

Go, gather together all the Jews that are present in Shushan, and fast ye for me, and neither eat nor drink three days, night or day: I also and my maidens will fast likewise; and so, will I go in unto the king, which is not according to the law: and if I perish, I perish (Esther 4:16).

SEVEN DAYS FAST

And they took their bones, and buried them under a tree at Jabesh, and fasted seven days (1 Samuel 31:13).

TEN DAYS FAST

Prove thy servants, I beseech thee, ten days; and let them give us pulse to eat, and water to drink (Daniel 1:12).

FOURTEEN DAYS FAST

And while the day was coming on, Paul besought them all to take meat, saying, this day is the fourteenth day that ye have tarried and continued fasting, having taken nothing (Acts 27:33).

TWENTY-ONE DAYS FAST

In the third year of Cyrus king of Persia a thing was revealed unto Daniel, whose name was called Belteshazzar; and the thing was true, but the time appointed was long: and he understood the thing, and had understanding of the vision. In those days, Daniel was mourning three full weeks. I ate no pleasant bread, neither came flesh nor wine in my mouth, neither did I anoint myself at all, till three whole weeks were fulfilled (Daniel 10:1-3).

FORTY DAYS FAST

Then was Jesus led up of the Spirit into the wilderness to be tempted by the devil. And when he had fasted forty days and forty nights, he was afterward a hungered (Matthew 4:1-2).

And he was there with the LORD forty days and forty nights; he did neither eat bread, nor drink water. And he wrote upon the tables the words of the covenant, the ten commandments (Exodus 34:28).

And the angel of the LORD came again the second time, and touched him, and said, Arise and eat; because the journey is too great for thee. And he arose, and did eat and drink, and went in the strength of that meat forty days and forty nights unto Horeb the mount of God (1 Kings 19:7).

HEALTH BENEFITS OF FASTING

Fasting is the practice of abstaining from food or drink for a specific period of time. It has been practiced for centuries for various reasons, including religious, cultural, and health purposes. In recent years, fasting has gained popularity for its potential health benefits beyond just weight loss. Research suggests that fasting can have a range of positive effects on the body and mind.

Here are some of the key ways in which fasting can benefit our health:

1. **Weight Loss and Improved Metabolic Health**: One of the most well-known benefits of fasting is weight loss. When you fast, your body uses stored fat for energy, leading to a reduction in overall body fat. Additionally, fasting can help improve metabolic health by reducing insulin resistance, lowering blood sugar levels, and decreasing inflammation. This can lead to a lower risk of type 2 diabetes and other metabolic disorders.

2. **Autophagy**: Fasting triggers a process called autophagy, which is the body's way of cleaning out damaged cells and regenerating new healthy ones. This cellular repair mechanism can help protect against various diseases, including cancer and neurodegenerative disorders. By promoting autophagy, fasting may enhance longevity and improve overall health

3. **Spiritual and Emotional Benefits:** Beyond the physical advantages, fasting is often associated with spiritual growth and emotional clarity. Many religious traditions incorporate fasting as a means of purification and self-reflection. This time of abstention can encourage individuals to focus on their spiritual lives, fostering a sense of peace and purpose. The discipline required to fast can also build willpower and self-control, attributes that are beneficial in many areas of life.

4. **Enhanced Brain Function:** Research indicates that fasting can have neuroprotective effects. It may stimulate the production of brain-derived neurotrophic factor (BDNF), a protein that supports neuron growth and function. Increased BDNF levels are linked to improved cognitive function, memory retention, and a reduced risk of conditions such as Alzheimer's disease. Furthermore, fasting may help reduce oxidative stress and in ammation in the brain, contributing to better mental clarity and focus.

5. **Heart Health:** Fasting has been shown to improve cardiovascular health by lowering blood pressure, reducing cholesterol levels, and decreasing triglycerides. These factors collectively contribute to a lower risk of heart disease. Additionally, fasting can enhance the body's ability to adapt to stress, which is beneficial for maintaining heart health over the long term.

6. **Mental Clarity and Emotional Resilience**: Many people feel more focused and mentally sharp during fasting. This could be due to the release of norepinephrine and other neurotransmitters that promote alertness. Moreover, fasting health and quality of life. However, individuals must approach fasting responsibly and consult with healthcare professionals, especially if they have underlying health conditions or are considering prolonged fasting.

Finally, fasting is more than just a dietary choice; it is a holistic practice that can yield numerous health benefits. Whether it's through weight loss, improved metabolic health, enhanced brain function, or spiritual growth, fasting offers a pathway to better overall well-being. As more research emerges, it is likely that the understanding of the benefits of fasting will continue to expand, making it a valuable tool for those seeking to improve their health and quality of life.

And it came to pass in the fifth year of Jehoiakim the son of Josiah king of Judah, in the ninth month, that they proclaimed a fast before the LORD to all the people in Jerusalem, and to all the people that came from the cities of Judah unto Jerusalem (Jeremiah 36:9). Sanctify ye a fast, call a solemn assembly, gather the elders and all the inhabitants of the land into the house of the LORD your God, and cry unto the LORD, Blow the trumpet in Zion, sanctify a fast, call a solemn assembly (Joel 2:14-15).

Chapter Three

ACCEPTABLE AND EFFECTIVE FASTING

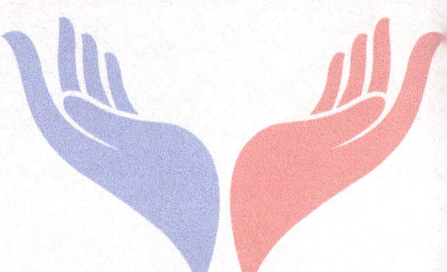

Isaiah 58: 1. Cry aloud, spare not, lift up thy voice like a trumpet, and shew my people their transgression, and the house of Jacob their sins.

2. Yet they seek me daily, and delight to know my ways, as a nation that did righteousness, and forsook not the ordinance of their God: they ask of me the ordinances of justice; they take delight in approaching God.

3. Wherefore have we fasted, say they, and thou seest not? Wherefore have we afflicted our soul, and thou takest no knowledge? Behold, on the day of your fast ye find pleasure, and exact all your labors.

4. Behold, ye fast for strife and debate, and to smite with the fist of wickedness: ye shall not fast as ye do this day, to make your voice to be heard on high.

5. Is it such a fast that I have chosen? A day for a man to afflict his soul? Is it to bow down his head as a bulrush, and to spread sackcloth and ashes under him? Will thou call this a fast, and an acceptable day to the LORD?

6. Is not this the fast that I have chosen? To lose the bands of wickedness, to undo the heavy burdens, and to let the oppressed go free, and that ye break every yoke?

7. Is it not to deal thy bread to the hungry, and that thou bring the poor that are cast out to thy house? When thou see the naked, that thou cover him; and that thou hide not thyself from thine own flesh?

8. Then shall thy light break forth as the morning, and thine health shall spring forth speedily: and thy righteousness shall go before thee; the glory of the LORD shall be thy rearward.

9. Then shalt thou call, and the LORD shall answer; thou shalt cry, and he shall say, Here I am. If thou take away from the midst of thee the yoke, the putting forth of the finger, and speaking vanity;

10. And if thou draw out thy soul to the hungry, and satisfy the afflicted soul; then shall thy light rise in obscurity, and thy darkness be as the noonday:

From the above scriptural verses, we can determine that not all fasting is effective and acceptable before the LORD. This is to show that fasting has spiritual guidelines that cannot be omitted or ignored! Therefore, it is important to follow biblical procedures to avoid wasting energy on counterproductive exercises. Fasting without proper spiritual direction is like speeding on the wrong side of the highway. Many believers experience lack of results because of anti-fasting practices!

Three categories of fasting exercises are:

1. Pre-fasting activities
2. Activities during fasting
3. Post-fasting activities

PRE-FASTING ACTIVITIES

For which of you, intending to build a tower, sitteth not down first, and counteth the cost, whether he have sufficient to finish it? Lest haply, after he has laid the foundation, and is not able to finish it, all that behold it begin to mock him, Saying, this man began to build, and was not able to finish (Luke 14:28-30).

These words of Jesus are profound statements: You need grace to engage in fasting adventures whether to begin or finish. What fuels the grace to start and finish a resultful fast is careful planning under the leadership -- inspiration of the Holy Spirit and revelation of God. Remember that the Scriptures are written by the inspiration of the Holy Spirit and revelation of God. You need the help of the Holy Spirit as the Spirit of Truth!

Another important part is that fasting opens the doors and gates of warfare both spiritually and physically: Or what king, going to make war against another king, sitteth not down first, and consulteth whether he would be able with ten thousand to meet him that cometh against him with twenty thousand? (Luke 14:31).

Here, you can begin to understand the need to start and finish your fasting with careful planning. Our planning is part of pre-fasting activities. Pre-fasting means the activities are not initiated in the midst or during your fasting period. Evaluation and estimation of every project is conducted before the commencement and not afterward.

All architectural designs are effective pre-project activities. It is dangerously risky to begin a building construction project before inviting a land surveyor, a quantity surveyor, and an architect. A Quantity surveyor is there to give you an approximation or estimation of how much it would cost, and what materials are needed to begin and successfully execute a building project.

The amount of money required to build a three-story building is not the same with building a stadium or bungalow. This is to emphasize that the LORD understands our individual differences and strengths. You must see His Love as a Father, and allow His Spirit to lead you in all things including but not limited to pre-fasting evaluations and analysis. Fasting is engaging in a spiritual project!

And Jehoshaphat feared, and set himself to seek the LORD, and proclaimed a fast throughout all Judah (2 Chronicles 20:3).

Chapter Four

BUILDING UP YOUR FAITH

But without faith it is impossible to please him: for he that cometh to God must believe that he is, and that he is a rewarder of them that diligently seek him (Hebrews 11:6).

Before you begin a fast, it is important to take a notebook or journal and carefully list all your expectations! Place the lists where you can easily look at the content as you fast and pray.

The Bible says, For surely there is an end; and thine expectation shall not be cut off (Proverbs 23:18).

You cannot effectively engage in fasting and prayers without setting defined goals. God never despises the expectations of His people, especially when they are within the context of His Will. The Will of God includes everything that pertains to life and godliness: salvation, Healing, deliverance, sanctification, consecration, restoration, power, wealth, health, mercy, grace, and favor, etc.

And I say unto you, Ask, and it shall be given you; seek, and ye shall find; knock, and it shall be opened unto you (Luke 11:9).

For every one that asketh receives; and he that seeks finds; and and to him that knocketh it shall be opened (Matthew 7:7).

Every expectation is fueled and powered by faith! The question is, how do you cultivate faith to receive from God?

1. YOU NEED THE WORD OF GOD

So, then faith cometh by hearing, and hearing by the word of God (Romans 10:17).

2. YOU NEED TO HEAR THE VOICE OF THE LORD GOD

Only if thou carefully hearken unto the voice of the LORD thy God, to observe to do all these commandments which I command thee this day (Deuteronomy 15:5).

The promises of God are plainly written in the Scriptures, so gather them together for your use:

1. You will need to write down the passages that talk about whatever you need from the LORD. Promises are for you to carefully retain the records for personal references, so that they become receipts or redeemable materials in your custody or possession.

2. You will need to memorize and recite the Words. Reading without retaining is like throwing away valuables. You will not only lose the ability to recover the materials but also give your opponent an advantage.

3. You are required to study and learn the Words. Studying is the secret to unlocking the keys of understanding. You are not only reading the Words to familiarize or become acquainted with the theories, but also to understand the application processes. Let him that read also understand (Mark 13:14).

4. You will need to bring the Words to the LORD's attention in your prayers. Referencing your requests and petitions before the LORD through prayers is like producing warranty and guarantee documents for services. You are holding Him to His Words, and you are saying I have all the written records in case you do not remember them.

But without faith it is impossible to please him: for he that cometh to God must believe that he is, and that he is a rewarder of them that diligently seek him (Hebrews 11:6).

Faith is a spiritual key or gateway that unlocks your desired expectations. However, the Word of God gives you the connecting links that help you to cultivate trust. The Bible said, So then faith cometh by hearing, and hearing by the word of God (Romans 10:17). The Word of God serves as a trigger mechanism because it holds the promises of God. Most importantly, the Word of God is the written Will, and to do His Will, you must know and understand the Will to apply it in your everyday life! If any man will do his will, he shall know of the doctrine... (John 7:17a).

Fasting and prayer are spiritual adventures that usher you into God's courts! And remember that every court is governed by written laws, decrees, and constitutions. You enter His gate with thanksgiving, and His court with praise but you are seated in His court for deliberations. This is why you must know the Word, so you may be able to carefully present your cases before the LORD. The Bible said, produce your cause, saith the LORD;

bring forth your strong reasons, saith the King of Jacob (Isaiah 41:21). You cannot have victory and favor in any court without proper presentations and representations. You need to incorporate the Word of God in your fasting and prayer, or simply before and during your periods of fasting and prayer.

Then I proclaimed a fast there, at the river of Ahava, that we might afflict ourselves before our God, to seek of him a right way for us, and for our little ones, and for all our substance (Ezra 8:21).

Chapter Five

LENGTHS AND TYPES OF FAST

We must depend on the leading of the Holy Spirit to influence our decision-making regarding all fasting and prayer arrangements. In chapter two we mentioned the different kinds of fasting, so you have to decide what works for your situation. You must also consider your strength as well as health. I understand that God's grace can override all our physical limitations.

The Bible says, Go, gather together all the Jews that are present in Shushan, and fast ye for me, and neither eat nor drink three days, night or day: I also and my maidens will fast likewise; and so, will I go in unto the king, which is not according to the law: and if I perish, I perish (Esther 4:16).

Esther and the people engaged in what we describe as a corporate fast and the length or duration of the fast was set for a period. You can decide on how long you want to fast, and you can also determine the nature of your fast. One of the advantages of knowing how long you want to fast will help you to properly schedule your activities.

You must have an open mindset and the reason is to allow for the Holy Spirit to lead you beyond the initial length or period of time you proposed to fast and pray if necessary. He will then release you after He has helped you to achieve your expected result or goal. On the other hand, if you desire to go on a long fasting period, you may need supervision -- a periodic check to ensure you do not harm your body in the process!

SCHEDULING A FAST

I want outline some Scriptures that validate careful planning and time management:

A person plans his way, but the LORD directs his steps (Proverbs 16:9).

But I will call on God, and the LORD will rescue me. Morning, noon, and night I cry out in my distress, and the LORD hears my voice (Psalms 55:16-17).

There is a season for everything, and a time for every event under heaven: a time to be born, and a time to die; a time to plant, and a time to uproot what was planted (Ecclesiastes 3:1-2).

So, then, be careful how you live. Do not be unwise but wise, making the best use of your time because the times are evil. Therefore, do not be foolish, but understand what the Lord's will is (Ephesians 5:15-17).

It is necessary to maintain the records of your schedules and table of activities during a fasting period. You can have a to-do-list or you can manually document a robust timetable to help you maximize your fasting and prayer experiences.

You may want to itemize such activities as time for:

1. Bible Study
2. Prayers
3. Rest
4. Meditation

You can also take inventory of your accessories, evaluate your action points as well as feedback, etc.

Go, gather together all the Jews that are present in Shushan, and fast ye for me, and neither eat nor drink three days, night or day: I also and my maidens will fast likewise; and so will I go in unto the king, which is not according to the law: and if I perish, I perish (Esther 4:16).

Chapter Six

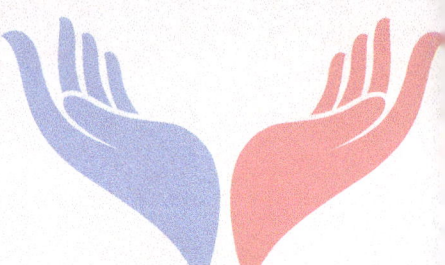

CHECKING YOUR HEART

Motives are extremely important when preparing for a fast, so you want to condition your heart and mind because you expect to receive from the LORD!

The Bible says, behold, ye fast for strife and debate, and to smite with the fist of wickedness: ye shall not fast as ye do this day, to make your voice to be heard on high (Isaiah 58:4).

In Matthew 5:23-24, we find: Therefore, if you are offering your gift at the altar and there remember that your brother or sister has something against you, leave your gift there in front of the altar. First go and be reconciled to them; then come and offer your gift.

But if you do not forgive other people, then your Father will not forgive your offenses (Matthew 6:15).

And when you pray, do not be like the hypocrites, for they love to pray standing in the synagogues and on the street corners to be seen by others. Truly I tell you, they have received their reward in full. But when you pray, go into your room, close the door and pray to your Father, who is unseen. Then your Father, who sees what is done in secret, will reward you. And when you pray, do not keep on babbling like pagans, for they think they will be heard because of their many words. Do not be like them, for your Father knows what you need before you ask him (Matthew 6:5-8 NIV).

When you fast, do not look somber as the hypocrites do, for they disfigure their faces to show others they are fasting. Truly I tell you, they have received their reward in full. But when you fast, put oil on your head and wash your face, so that it will not be obvious to others that you are fasting, but only to your Father, who is unseen; and your Father, who sees what is done in secret, will reward you (Matthew 6:16-18 NIV).

These aspects of fasting are so crucial because you have clear directions. If things go wrong, your efforts will be simply wasted. Therefore, you need to check your heart and ensure that you

sort out the following:

You must forgive those who offend you and apologize to those whom you offended. Secondly, you must be sure that there is no bitterness in your heart against anyone. If your heart is not pure before the LORD, satan can raise accusations against you and hinder your access to the Father. It does not matter what people have done to you. Learn to forgive them freely, especially when they take the steps to ask for your forgiveness. Your heavenly Father wants you to forgive them, so your access to Him will not be hindered.

Sometimes, it may be very difficult to forgive those who offend and hurt you deeply, but the Holy Spirit will help you to overcome your pain. You can bring these issues before the LORD to let Him know that you want to forgive. For some people, you may have to send them emails, and for some others, you might have to call on the phone or text to let them know you have made the decision to forgive them. However, for those whom you have offended, you may need to make some effort to apologize. If you are not able to contact them, talk to the LORD concerning the matters. You have to remember that He knows your heart as well as all your intentions or motives.

AVOID PUBLIC SHOWS AND APPLAUSE OF MEN

Whenever you fast and pray, you do not have to announce it everywhere. You want to be as private and focused as possible. Please, be discreet. Unless you are adhering to a Corporate Fast with a Church or Ministry, you must be very private. Fasting and prayer are not for proving points or showing anyone that you can fast. Read Isaiah Chapter 58. Public applause from men will cause the LORD's rewards to become elusive. You are fasting and praying for important reasons, and they should remain your primary focus until you achieve your goals. Avoid the temptations of the praises from men so that the LORD can bless and lift you up.

AVOIDING DISTRACTIONS

The light of the body is the eye: if therefore thine eye be single, thy whole body shall be full of light (Matthew 6:22).

You need a laser focus when you fast and pray. You may think that the enemy does not know when you are distracted. Importantly, it is difficult to lay hold on what belongs to you when you are.

Although the LORD can help us escape the trap of the enemy, you have a responsibility to put systems around your life to deflate or destroy the plans of the enemy against your life.

DISTRACTIONS COME IN MANY WAYS

It can be something like social media, friends, food, unfinished tasks, television, phone, and wondering thoughts, etc. There are so many ways that you can become distracted thereby giving the enemy an opportunity to take advantage of you.

Behold, ye fast for strife and debate, and to smite with the fist of wickedness: ye shall not fast as ye do this day, to make your voice to be heard on high. Is it such a fast that I have chosen? a day for a man to afflict his soul? is it to bow down his head as a bulrush, and to spread sackcloth and ashes under him? wilt thou call this a fast, and an acceptable day to the LORD? (Isaiah 58:4-5).

Chapter Seven

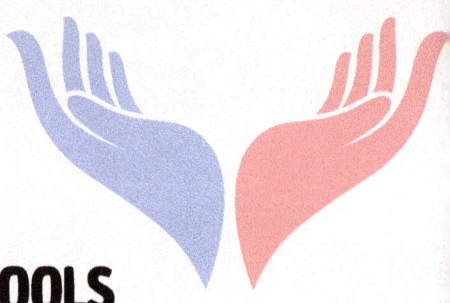

POWER TOOLS

Fasting, prayers, and studying the Bible are like threefold cords that cannot be easily broken. Here is a practical formula that I have personally adopted: Fasting plus prayers plus Bible Study equals to powerful results. Fasting is also a humbling experience and a tool for reshaping who we are, or what we represent.

The Bible says, because thine heart was tender, and thou hast humbled thyself before the LORD, when thou heardest what I spake against this place, and against the inhabitants thereof, that they should become a desolation and a curse, and hast rent thy clothes, and wept before me; I also have heard thee, saith the LORD (2 Kings 22:19).

If my people, which are called by my name, shall humble themselves, and pray, and seek my face, and turn from their wicked ways; then will I hear from heaven, and will forgive their sin, and will heal their land (2 Chronicles 7:14).

And when the LORD saw that they humbled themselves, the word of the LORD came to Shemaiah, saying, they have humbled themselves; therefore, I will not destroy them, but I will grant them some deliverance; and my wrath shall not be poured out upon Jerusalem by the hand of Shishak (2 Chronicles 12:7).

And when he humbled himself, the wrath of the LORD turned from him, that he would not destroy him altogether: and also, in Judah things went well (2 Chronicles 12:12).

Because thine heart was tender, and thou didst humble thyself before God, when thou heardest his words against this place, and against the inhabitants thereof, and humbledst thyself before me, and didst rend thy clothes, and weep before me; I have even heard thee also, saith the LORD (2 Chronicles 34:27).

When men are cast down, then thou shalt say, there is lifting up; and he shall save the humble person (Job 22:29).

Arise, O LORD; O God, lift up thine hand: forget not the humble (Psalms 10:12).

But as for me, when they were sick, my clothing was sackcloth: humbled my soul with fasting; and my prayer returned into mine own bosom (Psalms 35:13).

GOD RESISTS OR OPPOSES THE PROUD

But he giveth more grace. Wherefore he saith, God resisteth the proud, but giveth grace unto the humble (James 4:6).

Likewise, ye younger, submit yourselves unto the elder. Yea, all of you be subject one to another, and be clothed with humility: for God resisteth the proud, and giveth grace to the humble (1 Peter 5:5).

PRIDE IS PART OF THE WORKS OF THE FLESH SO THE ENEMY BENEFITS TO YOUR DISADVANTAGE

For all that is in the world, the lust of the flesh, and the lust of the eyes, and the pride of life, is not of the Father, but is of the world (1 John 2:16).

FASTING IS BRINGING YOUR BODY UNDER SUBJECTION

But I keep under my body, and bring it into subjection: lest that by any means, when I have preached to others, I myself should be a castaway (1 Corinthians 9:27).

PRIDE CAN MAKE YOUR FASTING IRRELEVANT BECAUSE GOD RESISTS OR OPPOSES THE PROUD

But he giveth more grace. Wherefore he saith, God resisteth the proud, but giveth grace unto the humble (James 4:6).

Likewise, ye younger, submit yourselves unto the elder. Yea, all of you be subject one to another, and be clothed with humility: for God resisteth the proud, and giveth grace to the humble (1 Peter 5:5).

One of the greatest advantages of fasting is that it facilitates the processes of liberating your spirit in the presence of God. The flesh loses its nature as you fast and pray. We also have to look at the importance of fasting and prayer in dealing with stubborn issues of life. Some problems are spiritual while some others are physical.

Jesus said, howbeit this kind goeth not out but by prayer and fasting (Matthew 17:21).

This Scripture verse implies that a particular kind of spiritual power or powers does not respond except by prayer and fasting, and of course, we need to incorporate the Word of God. Remember that Jesus taught the disciples' secret prayer protocols.

And it came to pass, that, as he was praying in a certain place, when he ceased, one of his disciples said unto him, Lord, teach us to pray, as John also taught his disciples. And he said unto them, when ye pray, say, Our Father which art in heaven, Hallowed be thy name. Thy kingdom come, thy will be done, on earth as it is in heaven (Luke 11:1-2).

Prayer is only effective when prayed according to the Will of God. Parts of the Will of God are written for us, so we have to know the written Testament of His Will! And we have to ask the Holy Spirit to help us to read and understand what is written in the Will. A will is binding document so we have to understand the legal implications.

For I know the thoughts that I think toward you, saith the LORD, thoughts of peace, and not of evil, to give you an expected end. Then shall ye call upon me, and ye shall go and pray unto me, and I will hearken unto you. And ye shall seek me, and find me, when ye shall search for me with all your heart. And I will be found of you, saith the LORD: and I will turn away your captivity, and I will gather you from all the nations, and from all the places whither I have driven you, saith the LORD; and I will bring you again into the place whence I caused you to be carried away captive (Jeremiah 29:11-14).

The thoughts of the LORD for you are captured in the pages of the Testament of His Will. You must read and study the Word and activate the promises by faith to work in your life.

So, then faith cometh by hearing, and hearing by the word of God (Romans 10:17).

But without faith it is impossible to please him: for he that cometh to God must believe that he is, and that he is a rewarder of them that diligently seek him (Hebrews 11:6).

In your fasting, it's imperative that you add Bible Studies, and to your Bible Studies, you must add prayers. These are essential keys to reaping the benefit of His great grace, power, blessings, and restoration. Fasting helps you to remain humble. The Word of God helps you to discover the Will of God for your life, and prayer reminds and provokes God to answer from Heaven.

Then came to him the disciples of John, saying, Why do we and the Pharisees fast oft, but thy disciples fast not? And Jesus said unto them, Can the children of the bridechamber mourn, as long as the bridegroom is with them? but the days will come, when the bridegroom shall be taken from them, and then shall they fast (Matthew 9:14-15).

Chapter Eight

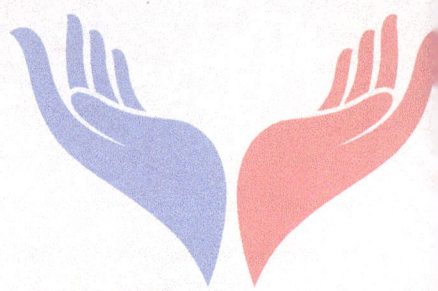

MEDITATION AND REST

During fasting, the physical body can lose a lot of nutrients even though the spirit man gains certain advantages, so it is important to get good rest.

And on the seventh day God ended his work which he had made; and he rested on the seventh day from all his work which he had made. And God blessed the seventh day, and sanctified it: because that in it he had rested from all his work which God created and made (Genesis 2:2-3).

God made provisions for rest through the idea of Sabbath:

And he said unto them, this is that which the LORD hath said, Tomorrow is the rest of the holy sabbath unto the LORD: bake that which ye will bake to day, and seethe that ye will seethe; and that which remaineth over lay up for you to be kept until the morning.

See, for that the LORD hath given you the sabbath, therefore he giveth you on the sixth day the bread of two days; abide ye every man in his place, let no man go out of his place on the seventh day (Exodus 16:23, 29).

Remember the sabbath day, to keep it holy. But the seventh day is the sabbath of the LORD thy God: in it thou shalt not do any work, thou, nor thy son, nor thy daughter, thy manservant, nor thy maidservant, nor thy cattle, nor thy stranger that is within thy gates:

For in six days the LORD made heaven and earth, the sea, and all that in them is, and rested the seventh day: wherefore the LORD blessed the sabbath day, and hallowed it (Exodus 20:8,10,11).

The Sabbath indicates rest! God factored this because He knows that the human body will break down without proper rest. Whenever you schedule your next fasting and prayer event, make sure you rest yourself through the process.

It is vain for you to rise up early, to sit up late, to eat the bread of sorrows: for so he giveth his beloved sleep (Psalms 127:2).

Refreshment and Rejuvenation

But ye are come unto mount Sion, and unto the city of the living God, the heavenly Jerusalem, and to an innumerable company of angels, to the general assembly and church of the firstborn, which are written in heaven, and to God the Judge of all, and to the spirits of just men made perfect, and to Jesus the mediator of the new covenant, and to the blood of sprinkling, that speaketh better things than that of Abel (Hebrews 12:22-23).

FASTING AND MEDITATION

And Isaac went out to meditate in the field at the eventide: and he lifted up his eyes, and saw, and, behold, the camels were coming (Genesis 24:16).

The word meditation means to focus one's mind for a period of time. It is a moment of silence or recitation for spiritual purposes or as a method of relaxation. Mediation is not an abstract event: the subject of meditation is pondering deeply on the Word of God.

The Bible says, this book of the law shall not depart out of thy mouth; but thou shalt meditate therein day and night, that thou mayest observe to do according to all that is written therein: for then thou shalt make thy way prosperous, and then thou shalt have good success (Joshua 1:8).

But his delight is in the law of the LORD; and in his law doth he meditate day and night (Psalms 1:2).

When I remember thee upon my bed, and meditate on thee in the night watches (Psalms 63:6).

I will meditate also of all thy work, and talk of thy doings (Psalms 77:12).

I will meditate in thy precepts, and have respect unto thy ways.

Princes also did sit and speak against me: but thy servant did meditate in thy statutes.

My hands also will lift up unto thy commandments, which I have loved; and I will meditate in thy statutes.

Mine eyes prevent the night watches, that I might meditate in thy word (Psalms 119:15, 23, 48, 148).

Meditate upon these things; give thyself wholly to them; that thy profiting may appear to all (1 Timothy 4:15).

Effects of Meditation:

1. Meditation helps to internalize the Word of God
2. Meditation helps to receive from God
3. Meditation provokes fellowship with the Holy Spirit

How to meditate as a believer:

- Look for a quiet and comfortable place free of distraction
- Prepare your mind and heart for prayer
- Ponder on the Words of His Promises
- Allow the LORD to fill your heart
- Finish with thanksgiving and appreciation

Accessories means external things you can have around to help you achieve a rich fasting and prayer experiences!

Here are some of the lists:

1. Bible

2. Music Player

3. Gospel Messages

4. Songs of Praise and Worship

5. Notepad

6. Pen

7. Notes of Instructions You May Have Received From the LORD

8. Lists of Your Expectations

9. Targeted Scriptures with God's Promises

10. Headphones or Bluetooth Speakers

Moreover when ye fast, be not, as the hypocrites, of a sad countenance: for they disfigure their faces, that they may appear unto men to fast. Verily I say unto you, They have their reward (Matthew 6:16).

Chapter Nine

ANGELS AND WARFARE

When we position ourselves to seek the face of God through fasting, prayers, and studying the Word of God, we are interacting with spiritual entities:

But ye are come unto mount Sion, and unto the city of the living God, the heavenly Jerusalem, and to an innumerable company of angels, to the general assembly and church of the firstborn, which are written in heaven, and to God the Judge of all, and to the spirits of just men made perfect, and to Jesus the mediator of the new covenant, and to the blood of sprinkling, that speaketh better things than that of Abel (Hebrews 12:22-24).

The word "angel" is derived from the Greek angelos (messenger). In New Testament Greek, the word took on the meaning "divine messenger, messenger of God." Var: Angel, Angell, Anzioleto, Anziolo. Angels are assigned with different respective roles!

Angels are deployed to attend to us when we pray:

In the third year of Cyrus king of Persia a thing was revealed unto Daniel, whose name was called Belteshazzar; and the thing was true, but the time appointed was long: and he understood the thing, and had understanding of the vision. In those days I Daniel was mourning three full weeks. I ate no pleasant bread, neither came flesh nor wine in my mouth, neither did I anoint myself at all, till three whole weeks were fulfilled. And in the four and twentieth day of the first month, as I was by the side of the great river, which is Hiddekel; Then I lifted up mine eyes, and looked, and behold a certain man clothed in linen, whose loins were girded with fine gold of Uphaz: His body also was like the beryl, and his face as the appearance of lightning, and his eyes as lamps of fire, and his arms and his feet like in color to polished brass, and the voice of his words like the voice of a multitude. And I, Daniel alone saw the vision: for the men that were with me saw not the vision; but a great quaking fell upon them, so that they fled to hide themselves. Therefore, I was left alone, and saw this great vision, and there remained no strength in me: for my comeliness was turned in me into corruption, and I retained no strength.

Yet I heard the voice of his words: and when I heard the voice of his words, then was I in a deep sleep on my face, and my face toward the ground. And, behold, a hand touched me, which set me upon my knees and upon the palms of my hands. And he said unto me, O Daniel, a man greatly beloved, understand the words that I speak unto thee, and stand upright: for unto thee am I now sent. And when he had spoken this word unto me, I stood trembling. Then he said unto me, Fear not, Daniel: for from the first day that thou didst set thine heart to understand, and to chasten thyself before thy God, thy words were heard, and I am come for thy words. But the prince of the kingdom of Persia withstood me one and twenty days: but, lo, Michael, one of the chief princes, came to help me; and I remained there with the kings of Persia. Now I am come to make thee understand what shall befall thy people in the latter days: for yet the vision is for many days. And when he had spoken such words unto me, I set my face toward the ground, and I became dumb. And, behold, one like the similitude of the sons of men touched my lips: then I opened my mouth, and spake, and said unto him that stood before me, O my lord, by the vision my sorrows are turned upon me, and I have retained no strength.

For how can the servant of this my lord talk with this my lord? For as for me, straightway there remained no strength in me, neither is there breath left in me. Then he came again and touched me one like the appearance of a man, and he strengthened me, and said, O man greatly beloved, fear not: peace be unto thee, be strong, yea, be strong. And when he had spoken unto me, I was strengthened, and said, let my lord speak; for thou hast strengthened me. Then said he, Knowest thou wherefore I come unto thee? And now will I return to fight with the prince of Persia: and when I am gone forth, lo, the prince of Grecia shall come. But I will shew thee that which is noted in the scripture of truth: and there is none that holdeth with me in these things, but Michael your prince (Daniel 10:1-21).

The LORD God heard the prayers of Daniel from the first day he began his fast, but demonic princes withstood the answers to his prayers. Nevertheless, his tenacity provoked the release of powerful angels to intervene. Your persistence puts the realms under pressure until Heaven responds. The same scenario applied to Peter when the people persisted in prayers until an angel came to release him from prison in Acts Chapter 12:1-19).

Do the following after every fasting and prayer, and never forget that obedience produces consistent result:

1. Maintain the culture of praying and studying the Word of God.
2. Keep away malice, hatred, resentment, and bitterness.
3. Cultivate and nurture the atmosphere of peace, joy, and love.
4. Act on the instructions the LORD had given to you while fasting and praying.

Then came to him the disciples of John, saying, Why do we and the Pharisees fast oft, but thy disciples fast not? And Jesus said unto them, Can the children of the bridechamber mourn, as long as the bridegroom is with them? but the days will come, when the bridegroom shall be taken from them, and then shall they fast (Matthew 9:14-15).

Chapter Ten

FASTING FOR FREEDOM

Always, I like to emphasize the important keys of fasting, whether it relates to answers to prayers for healing, deliverance, restitution, reparation, repatriation, and restoration, etc. Fasting as part of prayer, offers secrets to expedited and accelerated processes. The spiritual breakthrough comes with tremendous acceleration to break spiritual and physical barriers. To see a sudden or momentary response, there must be a shift — infiltration, and penetration of the defensive and security layers prohibiting or protecting the spiritual and physical realms.

Fasting is useful and effective in thinning the walling partition of human flesh and removing spiritual barricades or blockades. Until the spirit realms come together with the physical realms, the sudden outburst of spiritual phenomena cannot begin to emanate at an accelerated speed. What causes people to break down and give up are the long periods of waiting and endless expectations for the results of their prayers. They throw in their towels because they feel that nothing is happening. In the same way, the atmosphere of expectation breeds miracles, and lack of results breeds discouragement and disappointment. Empty hope is not a substitute for real answers. This is why religious activities are separate from true Christian experiences. The disciples came to Jesus and asked Him to teach them how to pray.

And it came to pass, that, as he was praying in a certain place, when he ceased, one of his disciples said unto him, Lord, teach us to pray, as John also taught his disciples (Luke 11:1).

Praying and receiving answers are different! Formalities are only exhibitions of religious practices with no recipe for definitive outcomes. The activities can become the only hope and people are forced or coerced to embrace empty religion. A dead system is established as an alternative to answering for the true spiritual experience; however, until we carefully discern, estimate, and appreciate the deep values of spiritual things beyond assessments, claims and confessions, belief, hope, and trust, there can be no real loyalty and faithfulness, which are the key ingredients of spiritual establishment. Empty prayers equal an empty life; therefore, satisfaction cannot be realized in the face of nothing. Building upon pretense will eventually lead to anxiety, debates, and extremism. Always, loyalty and faithfulness are not compatible with falsehood. The things we have no answers are things we cannot defend, and taking the matter into our own hands violates the spiritual order of life.

Many religious establishments are setbacks to people's destinies. Principles are parts of the codes to unlock a system or everybody will embark upon religious adventures, often with dangerous consequences. Although fasting is not starving, it is to curb the human appetite until spiritual transparency and clarity are achieved. The Will and purpose of God take more than rehearsing the Bible. There is an aspect of personal knowledge — or coming into real spiritual relations and experiences with the LORD God and no number of research and experimentation can suffice.

Any relationship at some point must involve personal interactions besides other engagements depending on the progression before the initial termination. To see the disciples address Jesus by the word "Master" is worthy of re-evaluation. We have religious prayers everywhere, but when it has to deal with praying and getting answered results, we do not have many masters. We have masters of theology and many other ideological concepts: political, religious, scientific, technological, and so forth! The human race is facing a dire moment.

We need those who will pray and make real contact with Heaven beyond touching the fabrics of man-made confusing and distracting systems. Prayer is a spiritual art; however, it is not ritualistic. It is simply attaining the pinnacle or climax of spiritual communication and dialogue. The most qualified ingredient of prayer is a combination of sacrifices and communications. The intrigue of prayers cannot be consummated until the answers to prayers begin to make landfalls in our lives. There is no way to keep records of achievements without the evidence of success.

Life is not programmed and animated (made/created) to accept complacency as an alternative to real success. Therefore, unanswered prayers provoke awareness of the loss of invested season, time, and effort. It is why we fight so hard to conceal the records of our failures in life.

The disciples acknowledged that Jesus was a Master in praying and seeing manifested and revealed answers. It would not be difficult to find people praying everywhere today if answers to their prayers were imminent. There would be protests to keep prayers in public places rather than to remove prayers from public places. We are seeing reversions of spiritual orders globally, not only in times of prayers but also the Church removing prayers from their gathering. We see the focus on more edifices, religious ceremonies, and coronations. We see empty benedictions, and pronunciations of blessings that never mature or manifest. We are seeing a pattern of the world systems and the Church systems pairing together like uniform codes.

Prayers mixed with fasting are important aspects of our lives as believers. If men ought to pray without fainting or until the answer to prayers is released, we must see the need for fervency, commitment, and dedication to prayers and fasting. It is the vehicle and practice that helps catapult our persistence in prayers. (See Luke 18:1). Spiritual strength comes from spiritual depth and fainting in prayer shows sudden relapse, disability, and other factors that paralyze the release of the atomic power of prayer. Anything that takes strength to achieve cannot take weakness to attain.

I am convinced in my heart that Jesus was giving away essential keys on how to invade spiritual spaces and realms by bringing down the overwhelming power of God in our lives. He was pointing to our ignorance about praying with variable — authenticating results. Leaving the scene of an important life-altering meeting is canceling the appointment, which means many people of God cancel their appointments with God because of a lack of fervent — enduring prayers that will win the case.

Answered prayers are parts of the sustainability of the Christian life or it's just as empty as other religions. Following after religion is opposing spiritual reality no matter how established the organization may be! It is written that "man shall not live by bread alone but by every word that proceeds out of the mouth of God." (See Luke 4:4). A true relationship is not a matter of paperwork or computer simulations. There are things which are written as there are those things that the LORD God is speaking even in the now. We must understand that the material equivalencies cannot override the necessity for spiritual balance.

For example, hearing Him speak has a different impact from reading every book about Him. If life itself is a love letter, the works of the cross would suffice the need for spiritual intimacy with the Holy Spirit, the glorified Christ, and the Father. Prayer is beyond all other forms of exhibitions as points of reference to connect us with Him.

There must be a burden — excruciating thirst, hunger, and deep passion in our hearts to persist and prostrate on the altar of prayer. It is the reason fasting is part of the birth of spiritual maturity. Spiritual growth and maturity are measured by how much flesh has been shed off until it is completely put off to enter the spirit realms. Fasting and prayer are like the contact of fuel and fire! Where the connections between the Spirit and the natural man fail to ignite a spark, thirst, and hunger for the outpouring must be used to draw the person closer. Spiritual deafness and blindness are not when the eyes are closed or when the ears are blocked; it's rather a spiritual phenomenon.

Proximity is determined by closeness or distance, so fasting and prayer close the distance -- bridging the gap to achieve closeness with the LORD. The closeness is the secret to consummating spiritual intimacy with Him. Absent in the body is present with the LORD: the closer we are to Him, the greater distance we achieve away from the world and the demonic powers. Always, the consistency of spiritual closeness is achieved through fasting and prayer. Putting off the flesh can only be achieved in two ways: by physical death, and personal surrender, submission, and whole sacrifice. (See Hebrews 9:14).

The perfect Will of God is received in the state of spiritual positioning. Most importantly, the depth of spiritual problems and addictions is also countered by the depth of the spiritual position. This is why there are besetting issues in peoples' lives and until they reach a certain spiritual threshold, the resolution of the matter will remain on hold. Besetting sins are controlling in nature; like retraction, they draw our movements backward to hinder or stop our progress and momentum!

Often, people would say things like:

1. I have done everything but I cannot break free, so I am just going to let the problem remain
2. I don't want to do this but I cannot help myself
3. I just can't find the answer so I am stuck

Our desires and actions are subject to change; however, many of us conclude that we are powerless — weak and tired, so we cannot achieve our breakthrough.

You must never surrender your will to the enemy. If satan can control your thought life, he can control your life. Our soul and body can also be impacted. Our lives can be turned upside-down when we believe the deception and lies of the enemy. We will begin to think how could we ever break free from our captivity and bondage? We start to wonder if we'll ever be able to regain control of our lives again. When we move to take control of our physical craving desires, we can develop inner strength to rise above the controlling power.

Fasting and prayer are fighting for control of your life. By taking control of your eating habits, you are dedicating, committing, and offering or sacrificing your life for the Will and purpose of God. When you fast, you are giving up necessary or enjoyable food as a demonstration, and you are standing against the forces that have taken your spiritual and physical cravings or desires captive. The way to diminish the physical craving desires is by spiritual strength and not by might nor by power. (See Zechariah 4:6). The Bible says, I can do all things through Christ which strengthens me (Philippians 4:13). Many believers go to the LORD with the notion that He will do everything for them. However, every walk of freedom takes personal endurance. God will never do everything for us because there is a requirement for our decisive participation and engagement. He did not create us so that He would control us like robots. He gave us free will to accept or reject Him and His proposals.

We either obey or disobey His Will and ignore His voice. He wants us to work out our salvation — go through the process to be made whole. He wants us to do our part of the work to realize our deliverance and freedom.

The Bible said, Wherefore, my beloved, as ye have always obeyed, not as in my presence only, but now much more in my absence, work out your own salvation with fear and trembling (Philippians 2:12).

Consistent fasting and prayers are the keys to breaking stubborn resistance, so you must learn to commit yourself continuously to fasting and praying until you achieve your breakthrough. Jesus said, this kind does not go out except by prayer and fasting (Matthew 17:21). Sometimes, we pray and the answer is released immediately. Other times, we may have to remain asking, seeking, and knocking until the answer is given to us. Discipline comes with great determination and expectations.

Important Steps to Take During Fasting and Prayers:

The first step is to decide what type of fast and the length or how long the fast will last. If you are going to embark upon more frequent fasting, you will have to pen down the days you will fast. Once you are set with these arrangements, you must endeavor to accomplish the goal. To break free from spiritual captivity and bondage, we must follow all the strategies that the LORD God has directed us. Deeper roots can infiltrate and penetrate our subconscious and impact our emotions, minds, and will — to affect our desires and behaviors.

The Bible said, For though we walk in the flesh, we do not war after the flesh: (For the weapons of our warfare are not carnal, but mighty through God to the pulling down of strong holds;) Casting down imaginations, and every high thing that exalteth itself against the knowledge of God, and bringing into captivity every thought to the obedience of Christ; And having in a readiness to revenge all disobedience, when your obedience is fulfilled (2 Corinthians 10:3-6).

We Must Denounce and Renounce All False influences and Controls:

We must have the ability to know the false and the counterfeit. You need discernment of spirits, the inspiration of the Spirit, and the revelation of God. Many people will be victimized and exploited in the end times as they err from the truth. They will accept the counterfeit and expose themselves to the false.

The Bible said, But I fear, lest by any means, as the serpent beguiled Eve through his subtlety, so your minds should be corrupted from the simplicity that is in Christ (2 Corinthians 11:3).

There are many counterfeiters today, and we are faced with great falsehood everywhere. Darkness is covering the world and gross darkness is covering the people. Errors are everywhere and people are deceiving and being deceived. The choices of books, movies, music, and websites we visit can easily entangle our lives. People are consciously and unconsciously opening their lives to the occult, New Age, black, and white magic as well as other false religions.

John 10:10a said, the thief cometh not, but for to steal, and to kill, and to destroy.

We Must Deal with All Deception and Lies:

Both self and outside deception share a common outcome. We are simply deceived, and we need the truth. The truth is very important to receive our deliverance and freedom.

Psalms 51:6 said, Behold, thou desirest truth in the inward parts: and in the hidden part You shalt make me to know wisdom.

Some of the ways we fall into deception are:

We deceive ourselves when we hear the Word of the LORD God and fail to live by or do the Word:

And he answered and said unto them, my Mother and my brethren are these which hear the word of God, and do it Luke 8:21) .

But be ye doers of the word, and not hearers only, deceiving your own selves (James 1:22).

Therefore, to him that knows to do good, and doeth it not, to him it is sin (James 4:17).

We deceive ourselves when we hide, cover, or deny our sins:

He that covers his sins shall not prosper: but whoso confesses and forsakes them shall have mercy (Proverbs 28:13).

If we say that we have no sin, we deceive ourselves, and the truth is not in us. If we confess our sins, he is faithful and just to forgive us our sins, and to cleanse us from all unrighteousness. If we say that we have not sinned, we make him a liar, and his word is not in us (1 John 1:8-10).

We deceive ourselves when we wrongly estimate and appreciate our valuable worth, exalt ourselves, and make ourselves who we are not:

And whosoever shall exalt himself shall be abased; and he that shall humble himself shall be exalted (Matthew 23:12).

For if a man think himself to be something, when he is nothing, he deceiveth himself (Galatians 6:3).

We deceive ourselves when we use the world as our measuring standards: When we evaluate and estimate ourselves by the standards of the world instead of the LORD God, we fall into deception and lies of the enemy:

The Bible says, let no man deceive himself. If any man among you seems to be wise in this world, let him become a fool, that he may be wise. For the wisdom of this world is foolishness with God. For it is written, He taketh the wise in their own craftiness (1 Corinthians 3:18-19).

We deceive ourselves when we think we can escape the consequences of our sins. Always, deception and bondage go together:

The Bible says, and ye shall know the truth, and the truth shall make you free (John 8:32).

Know ye not that the unrighteous shall not inherit the kingdom of God? Be not deceived: neither fornicators, nor idolaters, nor adulterers, nor effeminate, nor abusers of themselves with mankind, nor thieves, nor covetous, nor drunkards, nor revilers, nor extortioners, shall inherit the kingdom of God. And such were some of you: but ye are washed, but ye are sanctified, but ye are justified in the name of the Lord Jesus, and by the Spirit of our God (1 Corinthians 6:9-11).

We Must Forgive Others: When we choose not to forgive others, we put ourselves in spiritual bondage and sin. Forgiveness is a personal decision; however, we need the help of the Holy Spirit to forgive others after they have wronged us. The LORD requires us to forgive others; therefore, forgiveness is mandatory in our Christian life. When we forgive others, we also experience God's forgiveness in our own lives. True forgiveness is a remedial prescription and cure.

Apostle Paul wrote: To whom ye forgive anything, I forgive also: for if I forgave anything, to whom I forgave it, for your sakes forgave I it in the person of Christ; Lest Satan should get an advantage of us: for we are not ignorant of his devices 2 Corinthians 2:10-11).

You Must Submit to God's Authority: Submitting to God's authority and placing yourself under those He has raised up to lead you is part of dealing with personal rebellion. Authority and power always respect authority and power because it understands authority and power. Please see the case of the centurion (Matthew 8:8-10). We must subject ourselves under different chains of authority and power that the LORD God has appointed over us.

We are biblically commanded to submit to:

To the LORD God: We have sinned, and have committed iniquity, and have done wickedly, and have rebelled, even by departing from thy precepts and from thy judgments: To the Lord our God belong mercies and forgiveness, though we have rebelled against him (Daniel 9:5, 9).

Civil Governments: Let every soul be subject unto the higher powers. For there is no power but of God: the powers that be are ordained of God. Whosoever therefore resisteth the power, resisteth the ordinance of God: and they that resist shall receive to themselves damnation. For rulers are not a terror to good works, but to evil. Wilt thou then not be afraid of the power? Do that which is good, and thou shalt have praise of the same: For he is the minister of God to thee for good. But if thou do that which is evil, be afraid; for he beareth not the sword in vain: for he is the minister of God, a revenger to execute wrath upon him that doeth evil. Wherefore ye must needs be subject, not only for wrath, but also for conscience's sake. For this cause pay ye tribute also: for they are God's ministers, attending continually upon this very thing. Render therefore to all their dues: tribute to whom tribute is due; custom to whom custom; fear to whom fear; honor to whom honor (Romans 13:1-7).

Our Church Leadership: Obey them that have the rule over you, and submit yourselves: for they watch for your souls, as they that must give account, that they may do it with joy, and not with grief: for that is unprofitable for you (Hebrews 13:17).

Our Parents:Children, obey your parents in the Lord: for this is right. Honor thy father and mother; (which is the first commandment with promise;) That it may be well with thee, and thou mayest live long on the earth (Ephesians 6:1-3).

Our Employers: Submit yourselves to every ordinance of man for the Lord's sake: whether it be to the king, as supreme; Or unto governors, as unto them that are sent by him for the punishment of evildoers, and for the praise of them that do well.

For so is the will of God, that with well doing ye may put to silence the ignorance of foolish men: As free, and not using your liberty for a cloke of maliciousness, but as the servants of God. Honor all men. Love the brotherhood. Fear God. Honor the king. Servants, be subject to your masters with all fear; not only to the good and gentle, but also to the froward. For this is thankworthy, if a man for conscience toward God endure grief, suffering wrongfully (1 Peter 2:15-19).

Our Husbands: Likewise, ye wives, be in subjection to your own husbands; that, if any obey not the word, they also may without the word be won by the conversation of the wives; While they behold your chaste conversation coupled with fear. Whose adorning let it not be that outward adorning of plaiting the hair, and of wearing of gold, or of putting on of apparel; But let it be the hidden man of the heart, in that which is not corruptible, even the ornament of a meek and quiet spirit, which is in the sight of God of great price (1 Peter 3:1-4).

We are personally responsible for the things we do even if we are coerced, tempted, or deceived by others. Therefore, we must endeavor to take appropriate steps to remedy the situations before we can begin to realize normalcy in our lives. Pride is the enemy of personal responsibility. We must accept the responsibility for our situations. Pride and self-exaltation can lead to captivity and bondage. If the Son therefore shall make you free, ye shall be free indeed (John 8:36); however, freedom is never passive.

There are works on the part of the Savior as well as those being saved. Wherefore, my beloved, as ye have always obeyed, not as in my presence only, but now much more in my absence, work out your own salvation with fear and trembling (Philippians 2:12). Surrendering and submitting to Jesus Christ and the Holy Spirit are active engagements, and we can exercise our free-will to obey or disobey the law and the voice of the LORD God. Always, the confession of our sins is mandatory. If we say that we have no sin, we deceive ourselves, and the truth is not in us.

If we confess our sins, he is faithful and just to forgive us our sins, and to cleanse us from all unrighteousness (1 John 1:8-9). Sometimes, we mistake repentance for a pause. Nevertheless, admitting our wrongs is taking full responsibility instead of passing the blame to others. (See Genesis 3:12-13). Some people think that repentance is a formality: they repeatedly confess their sins, but immediately turn back to the same behaviors. Often, the reason is because of bondage. Addiction is part of bondage as sin is part of addiction. Sin leads to captivity and bondage in the lives of the people of God. The formalities of repentance can only lead to more excuses or tolerance for the same behaviors.

The Bible says, neither yield ye your members as instruments of unrighteousness unto sin: but yield yourselves unto God, as those that are alive from the dead, and your members as instruments of righteousness unto God (Romans 6:13).

Responsibility is part of humility; therefore, when we take responsibility for our sins, we humble ourselves before the LORD to secure the release and freedom we desire.

Disassociation is a component of true repentance because evil communication corrupts good manners. Some friends and acquaintances are snares on your path of life. Every individual is predisposed to certain behavioral characteristics, often emanating from different sources.

They could be related but not limited to:

- Emotional/mental or psychological issues
- Genetics/background or foundational problems
- Sin, trespass, iniquity, and transgression
- People we follow or those who influence us
- Satanic or demonic activities

We must reject becoming a part of other people's sins and cut off their influences over our lives including family history. (See Exodus 20:4-5; Gal. 5:24). Bible promises are fundamental in possessing our inheritance, so we must acknowledge the written records and prayerfully ask for the release of the blessings. Scriptures are fulfilled through fasting and prayers — the Holy Spirit moves to bring the realities into our lives.

These Scriptures will help you in your prayers:

For ye are bought with a price: therefore, glorify God in your body, and in your spirit, which are God's (1 Corinthians 6:20).

And they that are Christ's have crucified the flesh with the affections and lusts (Galatians 5:24).

But God, who is rich in mercy, for his great love wherewith he loved us, even when we were dead in sins, hath quickened us together with Christ, (by grace ye are saved;) And hath raised us up together, and made us sit together in heavenly places in Christ Jesus (Ephesians 2:4-6).

But if we walk in the light, as he is in the light, we have fellowship one with another, and the blood of Jesus Christ his Son cleanseth us from all sin (1 John 1:7).

Here are some key points to remember:

1. Renunciation and denunciation.
2. Acknowledgment and repentance of all your sins, transgressions, iniquities, trespasses, offenses, and faults.
3. Forgiving others who have wronged you and praying for them.
4. Surrendering yourself and submitting to the guidance of the Holy Spirit.
5. Separating yourself from the company of evil people.

Responsibility is taking important steps to address critical issues in your life. Fasting and prayer trigger spiritual warfare, so people face additional challenges when they try to fast. The Bible says, howbeit this kind goes not out but by prayer and fasting (Matthew 17:21). In spiritual warfare, you must exercise diligent caution to utilize all available weapons to defeat your enemy. Warfare always takes strategy including designed plans! Please see Isaiah 58:1-14.

I must conclude here that, it takes a great appetite to achieve deep focus on prayer. Often, we treat prayers casually because it is not exciting or involve several numbers of people cheering together. The atmosphere of prayer requires seclusion unless it is in a corporate setting; therefore, certain attractions for prayer are lost from the very start. Not everyone wants to commit to hours of prayer although it is the biblical clinical remedies or prescriptions for cultivating lasting discipline and spiritual endurance. For some people, prayers are their last options instead of gravitating towards the appealing or summoning of the Holy Spirit for prayers.

Many churches have no prayer events regardless of endless enticing programs. Choosing the path of entertainment has led to powerlessness and spiritual bankruptcy among church-goers. The reasons why people attend churches are not necessarily for social purposes or to belong to a social group. There are true seekers amongst the broad audiences that embrace the cultures of religious entertainment.

We have to know that hunger and thirst are purpose-driven, so there are underlining factors why people pursue after different respective goals. Spiritual awakening is a mobilization call, and until the people experienced resuscitation by the Holy Spirit, great expectations will be simply lost. Losing touch with reality is turning people into idols: our generation is in desperate need for spiritual life and power today. We may not know that the Christian life is sustained by prayer more than the air we breathe.

Nevertheless, some of us will assume that our coldness or lack of responsiveness are evidence of contemporary and modern Christianity, which in many cases are just carnal organizations. Like a fish cannot survive out of the water, a prayerless life is a wasted life. We need effective prayers in the churches today to fan the fires of revival because we are unconsciously entertaining the dead. Resurrection cannot happen without explosion of the Spirit of Life.

Energy takes discipline to cultivate, so we need strong men and women of God to carry the burdens of the work of the LORD. There are so much resting upon our shoulders because we are expected to bear the pressures of The End Times, and yet fulfill our God ordained commissions. We must see prayers as our oxygen to thrive in the midst of the dead valleys all around us.

Life is not casual so requirements are preconditions, and we must accept the conditions to meet the requirements.

There must be cries rising from every building and street! There must be an urgent mobilization and re-enforcement efforts to maintain the pressures until the altars of the LORD catches fire. When the fire comes, we will distinguish between the dead and the fakes. Revival is not a byproduct of falsehood: it is the fire of the LORD that exposes the uncircumcised hearts and flesh of men. The spirit and flesh do not mix and without a thorough spiritual checkup, the hearts of people are subtle. The LORD wants us to be baptized with the Holy Spirit and with fire to drive us to the altars of sanctification and consecration until we become living sacrifices like Shedrack, Meshack, and Abednego, who refused to bow before the idol image of King Nebukadnezar.

Prayer is the key to heart surgery in the spiritual realms and dimensions, and we are in a moment that we need a crossover now rather than later. My prayer is that this book will make a mark on your life, and create a new hunger and thirst for a true spiritual awakening in your spirit, soul, and body. He who hungers and thirst after righteousness shall be filled. The lifestyle of prayer and fasting has many spiritual and physical benefits.

It connects you to the Most important Source of Life -- the True Living God. "It is to your advantage that I go away; for if I do not go away, the Helper will not come to you; but if I depart, I will send Him to you." (See John 16:7). The Holy Spirit will enable you through the practice of prayer and fasting to fulfill the purpose of Heaven on Earth. May the Atomic Power of Fasting become your new weapon in your spiritual arsenal.

Dear Clients, Family, and Friends

As we embark on the journey of fasting together, I want to share some guidelines that will help you embrace this profound practice with both spiritual and physical awareness. Fasting is not just about abstaining from food; it's a holistic experience that can lead to deep personal transformation.

Here are the guidelines I encourage you to consider:

Set Your Intentions: Before you begin, take a moment to reflect on your hearts intentions for fasting. What do you hope to gain? Whether it's clarity, healing, or a deeper connection with the Lord, setting clear intentions will guide your journey.

Practice Forgiveness: I invite you to forgive those who have wronged you. Holding onto grudges creates emotional blockages that can hinder the spiritual benefits of your fast. Let go to make space for growth.

Incorporate Prayer and Meditation: Integrate regular prayer or meditation on scriptures into your fasting routine. This practice can enhance your mindfulness and deepen your spiritual connection with Christ.

Engage in Self-Reflection: Use this time for self-reflection. Keep a journal to document your thoughts, feelings, and experiences. This will help you process your emotions and gain valuable insights.

Cultivate Gratitude: Start a daily gratitude practice by listing things you are thankful for. Shifting your focus from what you're abstaining from to the abundance in your life can be incredibly uplifting.

Perform Acts of Kindness: During your fast, I encourage you to engage in acts of kindness. This not only elevates your spirit but also fosters a sense of community and connection with others.

Limit Distractions: Consider reducing distractions, such as social media or excessive television. Creating a sacred space for spiritual growth will allow you to focus on your journey.

Engage with Scripture: If it resonates with you, read spiritual texts that inspire you. These can offer guidance and encouragement during your fasting period.

Connect with Nature: Spend time in nature. The beauty of the natural world can nourish your spirit and provide a serene backdrop for reflection.

Seek Community Support: Remember, you are not alone on this journey. Engage with a supportive community for encouragement and accountability throughout your fasting experience. Here in our ministry, we fast often together, corporately it helps individuals press in towards their goals and aids each person to not give up, and reach the finish line.

Physical Guidelines

Consult with a Healthcare Professional: Before starting your fast, please discuss your plans with a healthcare professional, especially if you have underlying health conditions or are on medication. Your health is the priority.

Stay Hydrated: Hydration is essential. Drink plenty of water, coconut water is a great choice, before and after your fasting period to maintain your energy levels and overall health.

Transition Gradually: I recommend easing into your fast. Start by reducing your food intake or trying intermittent fasting methods to prepare your body.

Focus on Balanced Nutrition: Prior to fasting, ensure you eat balanced meals rich in nutrients. This will help sustain your energy during the fasting period.

Listen to Your Body: Pay close attention to how your body responds during the fast. If you experience any adverse effects, it's important to reassess and adjust your approach.

Prioritize Rest and Recovery: Rest is vital during fasting. Make sleep and relaxation a priority to support your physical and spiritual well-being.

Incorporate Light Exercise: Consider light exercise, such as walking or cycling.

FASTING GUIDELINES

Prior to beginning any type of fast, each participant should consult with his or her doctor.

As wonderful of a tool as fasting is for health and cleansing and detoxification purposes, there are some individuals who have certain conditions where fasting is contraindicated or prohibited.

Please keep the following in mind if you are considering the pursuit of a fast:

- Do not fast if you are pregnant or nursing.
- Do not fast if you have a serious illness like cancer, AIDS, Anorexia Nervosa, Leukemia, severe anemia, or if you are emaciated or malnourished as the result of another illness.

- Do not fast if you are a Type 1 Diabetic or Insulin-Dependent Diabetic.
- All Type II Diabetics (and some Type I Diabetics on insulin) should especially inquire of his or her physician about the feasibility of fasting and about any possible adjustments to the insulin/blood sugar-lowering medication regimen during the fasting period since the blood sugars tend to be lower during a fast. If diabetics receive medical clearance to do the fast, they should continue home monitoring of blood sugars throughout the fast as directed by their physician.
- Note: Of the options listed, The Daniel Fast is the most suitable option for Type II Diabetics, who have received medical clearance.
- Do not fast if you are taking a diuretic (or "water pill"). Diuretics precipitate loss of water and electrolytes like potassium. Do not fast if you have liver or kidney disease; the liver is the detoxifying organ of the body and the kidneys aid in the elimination of waste via the urine. If either of these organs is impaired, it will be difficult to obtain the usual benefits from fasting, and you may exacerbate your medical condition.
- Do not fast if you have congestive heart failure or a diagnosed cardiac arrhythmia. Do not fast if you are on certain medications like prednisone, narcotics, antidepressants, or diuretics. You should refrain from fasting if you are taking any of these medications. However,

there are other medications that can be safely taken during a fast. Please consult your health care provider when considering a fast to determine if fasting is right for you.

- Medications should not be discontinued abruptly. If a fasting participant is on medicine, he or she should consult his or her physician regarding possible adjustments to the medication regimen during the fasting regimen.
- If the participant develops exacerbation of an existing medical illness or begins to develop adverse reactions or worrisome symptoms of any kind, he or she should discontinue the fast immediately and consult his or her physician immediately.
- Distilled water is used for the Master Cleanser recipe; otherwise, if the faster is consuming water for hydration purposes with the other fasting options, spring or filtered water may be consumed.
- Organic produce should be used whenever possible where fruits and vegetables are listed in the fasting options.
- Fasters should be compassionate and gentle with themselves. During the fast, if they fall off the wagon and consume a restricted food or dietary item, they should acknowledge the detour (and enjoy it) and get back on the fast as soon as possible.
- How you end a fast is just as important as how you start and conduct one. A typical post-fasting regimen, for breaking a fast, would look like the following.

Starting with the first day after the fast:

Day 1: Eat fresh fruit, especially fruits with the highest water content because these are the easiest to digest and assimilate.
Note: On Day 1, avoid tropical fruits, such as pineapples and papayas, since these contain strong enzymes that might upset your stomach.
Day 2: You may have a combination of fresh fruits and vegetables throughout the day.
For instance, you might choose to have fresh fruit for breakfast followed by vegetable soup for lunch and dinner.
Day 3: You will follow a similar diet as outlined for Day 2.
Day 4: You may add to the various fruits and vegetable soups a salad and/or a baked potato.
Day 5: Building on the diet from the previous four days, you may now introduce a small serving of lean (preferably organic) meat, such as chicken, turkey or fish.

If you desire a DANIEL'S FAST SHOPPING LIST

Please read all labels before purchasing. Do not purchase foods containing refined sugars, excessive salt and/or additives. Please consult your doctor (especially those on medication) before you alter your diet or initiate a fast.

VEGETABLES

Avocados (avoid for weight loss), Leeks, Carrots, Yams, Bean Sprouts, Cabbage, Broccoli, Radishes, Beets, Peppers, Cucumber, Watercress, Potatoes, Squashes, Plantain, Egg Plant, Celery, Kohlrabi, Cauliflower, Zucchini, Peas, Turnips, Pumpkin, Brussels Sprouts, Onions, Sweet Potatoes, Parsnips, Artichokes, Asparagus, Tomatoes (limit because of acidity)

SALAD/GREEN LEAFY VEGETABLES

Romaine Lettuce, Chives, Lamb's Lettuce, Curly Endive, Oak Leaf, Butter Head Lettuce, Boston Lettuce, Radicchio, Watercress, Coriander, Spinach, Swiss Chard, Kale, Spinach Beet, Mixed Swiss Chard, Collard Greens, Cucumber, Chicory, Celery

FRUIT

Apples, Tangerines, Apricots, Grapes, Blackberries, Bananas (not during detox), Cherries, Lemons, Cranberries, Strawberries, Grapefruit, Pears, Plums, Greengages, Guavas, Pineapples, Melons (eat alone), Kiwi Fruit, Peaches, Mangoes, Star Fruit, Limes, Papaya, Currents, Cranberries, Gooseberries

BREADS/CEREAL

Spelt, Ezekiel (Bread and Pita), Pumpernickel, Sprouted Wheat/Grains (unbleached), Rye, Oat, Millet, Quinoa, Amaranth, Buckwheat, Wheat Germ

NUTS/GRAINS/SEEDS

Brown Rice, Basmati Rice, Almond, Sunflower, Pumpkin Seeds, Cashew, Sesame Seeds, Pistachio, Waleut, Brazil, Filbert (Hazel Nut), Macadamia, Pecan, Pine Nut, Brazil

HERBS/SPICES

Fresh Ginger, Garlic, Onions, Cilantro, Dill, Chives, Bay Leaves, Basil, Coriander, Oregano, Thyme, Parsley, Marjoram, Tarragon, Mint, Rosemary, Sage

LEGUMES/BEANS/SPROUTS

Adzuki Beans, Kidney Beans, Green Beans, Navy Beans, Pole Beans, String Beans, Lentils, Chick-Peas, Red Beans, Mung Beans, Broad Beans, Yam Beans, Wax Beans, Black-Eyed Beans, Butter Beans, Cannelloni Beans, Lima Beans, Pinto Beans, Haricot Beans, Soy Beans, Alfalfa Sprouts, Bean Sprouts, Broccoli Sprouts

DRIED FRUITS

Dates, Figs, Prunes, Raisons

Miso
Tamari
Soy Sauce
Vege-Sal
Braggs Liquid Aminos
Allspice
Cayenne Pepper
Cinnamon
Ginger
Cloves
Tofu Spreads
Mustard
Saffron
Sea Salt
Turmeric
Paprika

Balsamic Vinegar/Oil (makes a delicious salad dressing)

NON-DIARY

Almond Milk, Soy Milk, Rice Milk, Goat Cheese, Natural Yogurt, Hummus

DRINK LIST

Purified/Distilled Water (8 glasses), Herbal Teas, Fresh Vegetable Juices, Fresh Fruit Juices, Green Drinks, Hot Water & Lemon (upon rising)

SWEETNERS

Honey, Molasses, Stevia (natural sweetener from the Stevia flower)

OTHER

Free Roaming Hen Eggs, Sea Vegetables, Nori, Wakame, TVP (Texturized Vegetable Protein), Seitan, Tofu, Veggie Cheese, Olive Oil, Agar, Safflower Oil, Sesame Oil, Apple Cider Vinegar, Natural Mayonnaise, Fish, Ryvita Crackers, Ghee, Miso, Tempeh, Natto, Tahini, Roasted Barley (Coffee alternative), Sesame Butter, Smart Balance, Shoyo, Postum (Coffee alternative), Chicory (Coffee alternative)

SEASONING/CONDIMENTS

Other Natural Herbs and Spices

SUPPLEMENTS

Kelp
A Good Multivitamin

Garlic Tabs

Cayenne

Enzymes (consume with every meal)

Chromium Picolinate

Spectrobiotics (upon rising)

Olive Leaf

Grape Seed Extract

Noni Juice

Colloidal Minerals

Olive Oil (one tablespoon twice daily)

Oxy-Charge (add 7 drops to water 3 times a day)

LIVER TONIC

Black Grapes

Fresh Garlic/Garlic Tablets

Pure Carrot/Beet/Celery Juice (3 times per week)

KIDNEY TONIC

Cranberry Tablet Supplement

Hot Water/Honey/Braggs Apple Cider Vinegar (sip slowly)

Hot Water/Apple Cider Vinegar/Cayenne/Honey (sip slowly)

FOODS TO AVOID (do not eat!!!)

Refined Foods

Wheat/Wheat Products

Oranges (too acidic)

Avocado (those interested in weight loss)

Refined Breads

Coffee

Fried Foods

Latins

Red Meats

Chocolates

Shell Fish

Salt

Candy/Cakes/Cookies

Sodas

Chicken

Mushrooms (full of fungus)

Peanuts

Fast Foods

Spinach (if you are detoxing)

Carbonated Water

Processed Luncheon Meats

Dairy Products/Cow's Milk (full of steroids/growth hormones)

Ocean Spray Juices (they are not all 100%)

POWERFUL JUICE COMBINATIONS

1. Beet, Celery, and Alfalfa Sprouts
2. Cabbage, Celery, and Apple
3. Cabbage, Cucumber, Celery, Tomato, Spinach, and Basil
4. Tomato, Carrot, and Mint
5. Carrot, Celery, Watercress, Garlic, and Wheatgrass
6. Grapefruit, Orange, and Lemon
7. Beet, Parsley, Celery, Carrot, Mustard Greens, and Garlic
8. Beet, Celery, Dulse, and Carrot
9. Cucumber, Carrot, and Mint
10. Carrot, Celery, Parsley, Onion, Cabbage, and Sweet Basil
11. Carrot and Coconut Milk
12. Carrot, Broccoli, Lemon, and Cayenne
13. Carrot, Cauliflower, and Rosemary
14. Apple, Carrot, Radish, and Ginger
15. Apple, Pineapple, and Mint
16. Apple, Papaya, and Grapes
17. Papaya, Cranberries, and Apple
18. Grape, Cherry, and Apple
19. Watermelon (include seeds)
20. Leafy Greens, Broccoli, and Apple
21. Beets, Celery, and Carrots
22. Asparagus, Carrot, and Mint
23. Watercress, Cucumber, and Garlic
24. Mission Figs and Water
25. Your own favorite combinations

Note: During your juice fast, in addition to the above drinks, you may add the following beverages:

- Hot Water, Honey, Lemon and Cayenne Pepper
- · Herbal Teas
- · Aloe Vera (look for the fasting or detox formula)
- · Noni Juice

BE SURE TO CONSUME THE FOLLOWING ON A DAILY BASIS:

HOT WATER & LEMON   UPON RISING (alternate with Noni)
RAW VEGETABLES
WATER
FRESH FRUIT
FRESH GREEN SALAD
WHOLE GRAIN
BEANS/SEEDS/NUTS/GRAINS
PROTEIN
KELP SUPPLEMENT
MULTIVITMIN   (READ LABEL)
GARLIC TABS   (READ LABEL)
SPECTORBIOTICS
OLIVE LEAF,
COLOIDAL MINERALS
CAYENNE
CHROMIMUM PICOLINATE
FLAXSEED
NONI
with hot water & lemon)

Extended Thanks To:

Pastor Christian and Robin Harfouche, Pensacola, Florida. USA.

Apostle Victor Bessong, Boston Massachusset, USA.

Apostle Dan Effiong, Rain of Revival Ministries (A.K.A.) Revival Chapel, Nigeria, West Africa.

And many other precious men and women around the nation and around the world who devote their time and services to help others in need everywhere.

About The Author

Prophetess Dr. Evette Young was born and raised in New Orleans, Louisiana. She is a licensed and ordained Minister of the Gospel of Jesus Christ. She is the daughter of Mr. and Mrs. Emanuel and Evelyn Young. The wife of Dr. John K. Hill, and Mother of Anointed Evelyn Divine. She is an upcoming and a New Strong voice in the Kingdom of God. The power of God is extremely evident in her life and Ministry. Countless lives have been changed and transformed through her work. Dr. Evette is a prolific preacher who is empowered to release the fire of God. God has truly placed on her life the prophetic mantle, the working of the miraculous, healing, teaching, and preaching. She has an incredible deliverance power of God on her life to free people from addictions, sexual perversions, abusive relationships, all forms of demonic bondage, and satanic works, etc.

There are numerous testimonies and praise reports of bodies being healed and set free in her ministry. Dr. Evette is a tremendous, dynamic Woman of Prayer. She has impeccable integrity and lives a holy life unto the LORD. She is dedicated and committed to her God-given ministry assignment for the Kingdom of God. She has the Spirit of Excellence. She is a woman of class, servitude, and with uncanny boldness, she powerfully declares the unadulterated Gospel of Jesus Christ. Dr. Evette is a Graduate of World Harvest Bible College, where the Honorable Rod Parsley is founder and Pastor, and Graduate of International Miracle Institute, where Apostle Christian and Robin Harfouche are the Founders. She holds an AA, MA, PhD in theology. She has appeared on TCT Network, WACTV Live, World TV Network, and other Christian Networks. One of her goals is to rescue the little ones who are trapped in the sex trafficking industry. Part of her vision is to open a caring home to nurture and raise them in the love of our Heavenly Father and release them into their Kingdom Destiny! Dr. Evette teaches from the Kingdom perspective - on our Delegated Authority as citizens of Heaven.

One of her mandates is to awaken the appetite for the Glory of God within the hearts of the people of God.

She speaks primarily on operating as Kings and Priests, functioning in Dominion to subdue the earth and rule over it. Dr. Evette spends her life helping the discouraged, the disenfranchised, and those who have been emotionally wounded, abused, rejected, and bound by all kinds of bondage. Her drive is to empower God's people and help them discover their purposes and reach their full potential and experience true success in every area of their lives! Dr. Evette travels around the nation and the world, declaring the message of the gospel of Jesus Christ with authority and power. Her motivation is to challenge the people of God everywhere to reach for the higher realms and dimensions in their walk with Jesus Christ. Our ministry is passionately built to help others triumph through personal coaching, counseling, mentorship training, seminars, and workshops.

God's Royal Women Miracle Ministries is focused on helping women to know who they are, by learning how to value their unique contribution as women of class, honor, and dignity. Many women across the world are clueless about who they are in Christ. Some are struggling with identity crisis. Our endeavor is to bring spiritual insight and guide them with wisdom to maximize their full potential in Christ. Dr. Evette courageously pours her life out to help shape the lives of the downcast, bruised, wounded, and scared women using her own life's traumatic experiences. Her desire is to help men and women learn how to avoid the mistakes and the pitfalls that she walked through herself. Her message is purposed to bring deliverance and total healing and transform lives through the working power of Jesus Christ. Dr. Evette has a conviction to inspire other women to achieve true ladylikeness, which is in Christlikeness. Many women embark upon a search for the "real me" only to be deceived or frustrated to become whatever is the present-day image of a woman. True womanhood can never be measured by a man's affections, or societial praises, but by a woman's own character as defined and esteemed or appreciated by the Word of God.

There is no other standard for a true woman of God! And there is no reason why you should not become all that God has called and ordained you to be in life. We are a people of ministry. We know that ministry is finding the needs of the people and meeting them according to God's provision and supplies. We are working on building transitional housing for abused women and teenagers, and we are committed to clothing and distributing food to the less privileged or fortunate. The Bible said, by this my Father is glorified that you bear much fruit and so prove to be my disciples (John 15:8).

We are laborers in the Kingdom of God, effecting change in our nation and beyond! Our goal is to bring tremendous healing and whole prosperity to spiritually and physically thirsty and hungry. Dr. Evette Young will help you discover new strength to accelerate change in your quality of living, reforming dignity, reputation, and respect. We will show you how to overcome challenges and degree of difficulties of life, and how to rise above them!

Contact The Author

Dr. Evette Young

Address: 650 Poydras Street, Suite 1400,

New Orleans, LA 70130

Phone: 800.298.7262

Email: consult@transformationisnow.org

Online: www.transformationisnow.org

www.ingramcontent.com/pod-product-compliance
Ingram Content Group UK Ltd.
Pitfield, Milton Keynes, MK11 3LW, UK
UKHW021904240426
12048UKWH00044B/631